THE CATARACT OF LODORE

By Robert Southey

Illustrated by David Catrow

Henry Holt and Company ✦ New York

How does the Water
Come down at Lodore?"
My little boy asked me
Thus, once on a time;
And moreover he tasked me
To tell him in rhyme.

Anon at the word,
There first came one daughter
And then came another,
To second and third
The request of their brother,
And to hear how the water
Comes down at Lodore,
With its rush and its roar,
As many a time
They had seen it before.

So I told them in rhyme,
For of rhymes I had store:
And 'twas in my vocation
For their recreation
That so I should sing;

Because I was Laureate
To them and the King.

From its sources which well
In the Tarn on the fell;
From its fountains
In the mountains,
Its rills and its gills;
Through moss and through brake,
It runs and it creeps
For awhile, till it sleeps
In its own little lake.

And thence at departing,
Awakening and starting,
It runs through the reeds,
And away it proceeds,
Through meadow and glade,
In sun and in shade,
And through the wood-shelter,
Among crags in its flurry,
Helter-skelter,
Hurry-scurry.

Here it comes sparkling,
And there it lies darkling;

Now smoking and frothing
Its tumult and wrath in,
Till in this rapid race
On which it is bent,

It reaches the place
Of its steep descent.

The Cataract strong
Then plunges along,
Striking and raging
As if a war waging
Its caverns and rocks among:

Rising and leaping,
Sinking and creeping,
Swelling and sweeping,
Showering and springing,
Flying and flinging,
Writhing and ringing,
Eddying and whisking,
Spouting and frisking,
Turning and twisting,
Around and around,
With endless rebound!

Smiting and fighting,
A sight to delight in;
Confounding, astounding,
Dizzying and deafening the ear with its sound.

Collecting, projecting,
Receding and speeding,
And shocking and rocking,
And darting and parting,
And threading and spreading,
And whizzing and hissing,
And dripping and skipping,
And hitting and splitting,
And shining and twining,
And rattling and battling,
And shaking and quaking,
And pouring and roaring,
And waving and raving,
And tossing and crossing,
And flowing and going,
And running and stunning,
And foaming and roaming,
And dinning and spinning,
And dropping and hopping,
And working and jerking,
And guggling and struggling,
And heaving and cleaving,
And moaning and groaning;

And glittering and frittering,
And gathering and feathering,
And whitening and brightening,
And quivering and shivering,
And hurrying and scurrying,
And thundering and floundering;

Dividing and gliding and sliding,
And falling and brawling and sprawling,
And driving and riving and striving,
And sprinkling and twinkling and wrinkling,
And sounding and bounding and rounding,
And bubbling and troubling and doubling,
And grumbling and rumbling and tumbling,
And clattering and battering and shattering;

Retreating and beating and meeting and sheeting,
Delaying and straying and playing and spraying,
Advancing and prancing and glancing and dancing,
Recoiling, turmoiling and toiling and boiling,
And gleaming and streaming and steaming and beaming,
And rushing and flushing and brushing and gushing,
And flapping and rapping and clapping and slapping,
And curling and whirling and purling and twirling,
And thumping and plumping and bumping and jumping,
And dashing and flashing and splashing and clashing;

And so never ending, but always descending,
Sounds and motions for ever and ever are blending,
All at once and all o'er, with a mighty uproar,

And this way the Water comes down at Lodore.

To Deborah

Illustrator's Note

The Cataract of Lodore is located in the English Lake District, which is considered to have the most beautiful and varied scenery in the British Isles. Many poets and writers have made their home there, taking inspiration from its lovely waterfalls such as Lodore, its tarns and lakes, mountains and valleys, and old towns and villages. The area is also noted for its wildlife, including Canada geese, which were introduced from North America in the eighteenth century.

The name of the cataract, derived from the Middle English *low dore,* refers to the "door" between Borrowdale and Watendlath valleys where the falls plummet headlong into Lake Derwentwater.

I was inspired by Southey's words to celebrate in color and form the beauty of nature and the imagination of all children as they make their way from tarn to lake.

Illustrations copyright © 1992 by David Catrow.   All rights reserved, including the right to reproduce this book or portions thereof in any form.   Published by Henry Holt and Company, Inc., 115 West 18th Street, New York, New York 10011.   Published simultaneously in Canada by Fitzhenry & Whiteside Ltd., 91 Granton Drive, Richmond Hill, Ontario L4B 2N5.

Library of Congress Cataloging-in-Publication Data / Southey, Robert, 1774–1843.   The cataract of Lodore / by Robert Southey; illustrated by David Catrow.
Summary: At the request of his children, the author creates a descriptive poem evoking the sound and feel of water that flows on its way to a famous waterfall at Lodore in England.
ISBN 0-8050-1945-6 (alk. paper)   1. Waterfalls—Juvenile poetry.   2. Children's poetry, English.   [1. Waterfalls—Poetry.   2. English poetry.]   I. Catrow, David, ill.   II. Title.
PR5464.C38 1992 821'.7—dc20   91-29748   Printed in the United States of America on acid-free paper.∞   First edition   10 9 8 7 6 5 4 3 2 1